Our Ghosts Wait Patiently

poems by

Kathleen Goldblatt

Finishing Line Press
Georgetown, Kentucky

Our Ghosts Wait Patiently

Copyright © 2023 by Kathleen Goldblatt
ISBN 979-8-88838-097-0 First Edition
All rights reserved under International and Pan-American Copyright Conventions. No part of this book may be reproduced in any manner whatsoever without written permission from the publisher, except in the case of brief quotations embodied in critical articles and reviews.

ACKNOWLEDGMENTS

Grateful acknowledgement is made to the following publications where these poems or earlier versions of them first appeared:

Wickford Art Association: Poetry & Art: "Scratching Eggs," "Friday Morning, Ratiskovice"

The following poems have appeared in *Psychological Perspectives* 65 (1): "Leaving My Mother," "Father Tucked Away," "And This Is Love"

Publisher: Leah Huete de Maines
Editor: Christen Kincaid
Cover Art: Sam Goldblatt
Author Photo: Julie Brigidi, Oggi Photo
Cover Design: Elizabeth Maines McCleavy

Order online: www.finishinglinepress.com
also available on amazon.com

Author inquiries and mail orders:
Finishing Line Press
PO Box 1626
Georgetown, Kentucky 40324
USA

Table of Contents

I

Basement Kitchen 2
Lullaby 3
When I Was Seven 4
Before Church 5
Scratching Eggs 6
Broome County Airport, Summertime 7
The Field 8
And This Is Love 9
Great Uncle Gabriel 10
Gardening 11
Babička 12
Another Country 13

II

The Accordion 16
Every Monday 17
Dressing Up 18
Mass Before School 19
Sunday, Driving Home 20
Skating With My Older Brother in March 21
The Sleeping Porch 22
1963, Fourteen Years Old 23
The Fitting 24

III

The Visit 26
Leaving My Mother 27
Father Tucked Away 28
Pantoum For My Grandmother 29
Friday Morning, Ratíškovice 30
Old Town Square, Prague 31

For Eva Toman

*"Am I a combination of the lives of the ancestors? ...
do I embody these lives again?"*
C G Jung

I

Basement Kitchen

A metal-rimmed window at ground level,
smudged green by clotted grass from a hand mower.

A jam jar of ripe water on a dusty sill,
roots dangling beneath the bulb held by toothpicks.

A mustard yellow chair by the wood stove.

The dank sweetness of potatoes in one bushel,
apples in another.

Words have little power here.

Lullaby

She was making her way home—
she knew the road well yet
nothing was the same: the doctor had said there was
nothing he could do for that baby in her arms
so she turned around—

how much farther, her arms heavy now
how much farther, and no one could talk
when she arrived except a little girl
who played with the holy cards, who said,
that baby only smiles now.

Women wept and men did what men did
in the times when geese were fed in the yard.
Even after she was home, she kept walking
home with arms she could no longer feel
and heavy feet that shuffled.

When a baby flies past me—like lightning—
then disappears in the wind,
I remember her
and know that for a hundred years
weeping women don't stop.

It's then that I think she must still be walking,
singing her baby a lullaby, then another,
shushing her so that she may leave us all
to quiet—

When I was Seven

It's almost dinner time.

I sit in the wide-armed willow,
in the cave of its branches listening
to its whispering leaves.

My grandfather walks underneath with his friend.
I don't know why I sent for her,
I hear him say.

The corn grows tall and green.
The cabbage lies in clean straight rows.

The garden gate clangs shut.

I see my grandmother's dark red roses lace
the white trellis he has built for her.

Did the shade of the tree now long gone
know if she was ever his beloved?

Before Church

She puts on her black pillbox hat.
Takes the brooch from the milk glass dish,
pins it at her throat.

I sit on the bed watching.
She nods at my reflection in the mirror.
My mother calls her from the kitchen.

I open dresser drawers one at a time.
The top drawer: pressed handkerchiefs.
Bleached and frayed. Another rosary. Cotton underwear.

The next drawer: Flannel nightgowns,
worn out brassieres, six rows of hooks.
Hand sewn aprons.

The drawers smell clean,
everything ironed.
Layers of folded fabric in the bottom drawer, the deepest one.

Bay leaf scattered, old bits of dry moth in the corner.
Yellowed paper: I pull out a bundle of papers, photos—faces
long gone. Writing in a formal script.

A language I can't read.
Will I find more of her here?

I put everything back, carefully.

Scratching Eggs

Grandma puts away the dinner dishes, places newspaper
over the old tablecloth, brings out her green-shaded brass
lamp and a carton of hard-boiled eggs she has dyed purple–

so dark it is almost black–emerald green and turquoise.
She takes out her three-sided steel files,
puts on her silver-rimmed bifocals.

A delicate outline appears on the egg
until the whole surface is intricately covered:
flowers and leaves, uniform, precise, symmetrical.

I can tell she is happy as she works.
I do not know if she is a happy person—
her short, thinning gray-blonde hair

always in a net, except for Sundays,
her apron with its large pockets in the front,
bright light dancing off her bifocals.

She never takes her eyes off the egg.
I get the eggs she cracks by accident.
Hold them in my left hand

as she does, take the steel file in my right
like a pencil, and scrape the dye
in the shape of a flower.
Again and again my egg will break.
Again and again, she'll say "no 'no, fhats
okay, try agen." 'no, short for yes in Czech.

Broome County Airport, Summertime

He's out of the shoe factory at 4:00, home by 4:15,
changes into baggy pants, puts on his brown fedora,
the one that hangs inside the garage door, soft,
the way they get after years of being crumpled or
lost on the floor of the back seat. He forgets
where he puts it; my grandmother won't remind him anymore.

We get in the old Buick.
He drives peering over the steering wheel,
the way old men do even though he's tall,
his hands on the wheel are lined with black dye.

The small parking lot almost empty.
Grandpa gives me a hoist on the chain link fence,
helps me balance to get a toe grip.
Holds me while we wait.

A plane moves towards us.
Propellers rev until they're hummingbird wings.
I hold my breath. I'm never sure
it will turn, then lift.
I hold my ears against the roar,
imagine important people
behind the little windows looking down.

I cling to his shirt. He slaps his knee
without losing me.
Then he's somewhere else.

The Field

A gunshot across the field.
Grandfather's dark green boots
come around the shed.
My stomach hardens.
He looks straight ahead,
carries a heavy, drooping sack.

Later my mother calls for lunch.
I hear the chickens cluck to the clop of grandfather's boots
as he spreads feed in the yard.
Though I know there is no vet to call,
all day I cannot look near
the old man I love.
Nor the next.

But today on the porch, fifty years later,
with my own dog's head in my lap,
my grandfather could tell me
how he had seen the eyes
of his dog beseeching him,
that quiet man who taught me
to care for the garden and
tend the things that matter.

We make peace.
Our ghosts do not need to be called,
they wait patiently
for our attention.

And This Is Love

One dark suit in the back of the closet,
his slippers next to her black lace-up shoes.

She can still smell him when she opens the door.

The small bedroom is reflected in the beveled mirror,
its edges thin, blackened now.

She smooths the hem of her Sunday dress,
pins her hat.

The first time he left, a lifetime ago
to start a new life, factories were hiring.

Three years later, she had no choice.
She followed with one child,

the other left behind in the ground.

Her dresses hang above his brown shoes.

Great Uncle Gabriel

Are you sitting under a tree on a webbed folding chair?

Are you again filling my cup, again smiling at me with your hazel eyes?

A roast turns on the spit.
    Your wife hollers out the kitchen window,
                         more chairs!

Women scurry.
                Baskets of rolls.
    Plates. Plastic silverware.

Pastries cool on tables in the basement.

                Ivy climbs
  the stucco of your house.

My father plays his accordion
    in a sweat-soaked shirt.
His friend plays a French horn even louder.

We run to you.
You pick up the ginger ale
    with one large, veined hand, hold my tiny dixie cup
    with the other,
    pour.

Again and again.

Again and again.

Gardening

It's what I have left of you:
a battered pot hanging
in my shed by a hole in its handle.

When I pick it up, I'm gardening
with you.

You used it to scoop chicken feed.
When you were too old to have chickens,
used it to feed the stray cat that lived in your shed.

When I'm done scooping dirt, I hang it again
near the well-hewn door with its shiny latch.
I can see you smiling,

dreaming of me and whistling.

Babička

She stands on the porch,
hands dug into oversized pockets.

The smell of dill
through the kitchen door
of the small white house.

She watches us run through the grass
clucking like the chickens in her yard—
too loud. Too messy. Careless.

She'll always stand there,
waiting.

Another Country

Grandmother walks in from another room
and tells me to stop working, something
she would never say when she was alive.

I close the file, put away the book,
smell the dumpling soup she has made.
Her dirty apron no longer embarrasses me.

I accept the cup she offers,
her fingers still dusted with flour.

Rounded consonants roll off her tongue.
Her hollowed-out vowels soothe me.

We linger until my soup grows cold.
I hear only my own voice.

II

The Accordion

I pretend to know how to dance.

If I keep twirling to the count of three,
hopping a little as I put my head back
and smile, it looks like the polka.

If I spin fast enough my skirt
swirls out from my body.

My father sits on the bar stool,
balancing his accordion across his lap,

playing and singing without ever looking
at any of the small round pearl button keys,

light bouncing off the black lacquer,
his name set in rhinestones across the front.

No matter how fast I dance he never sees me.
He's looking somewhere I can never go.

Every Monday

From the back porch, the clothesline
is tethered to the house.

From this side of the sheets,
I see my mother's slim legs.

She pins his shirt,
reaching slowly overhead.

I know her lips are straight,
drawn tight.

Dressing Up

I take the box from the basement shelf,
lift the cream lace dress, step into it.

Twenty-eight pearl-sized covered buttons down the back.
 I only fasten a few.

What will I look like in my dress someday?

The long skirt is frayed at the bottom.
From dancing with my father?

A sepia-tone picture shows orange blossoms in her auburn hair,
a cascade of roses in her hands, smiles on both their faces.

One day the box is gone.
I know not to ask.

She would only shrug her shoulders, turn away
without a word.

Mass Before School

Boys on the right, girls on the left.

The bells ring three times.
The priest behind the altar raises the host, the chalice.

On the tall wooden crucifix behind him,
Jesus's face is frozen in anguish.

Mary on the left in a small altar,
she stands tall, arms open, palms up,
a vase of white lilies at her feet.

I sit and stare, wanting her lips to move.

She looks away.

Sunday, Driving Home

We sit in the backseat
of the smoke-filled Buick.

Mother looks through
her reflection in the passenger window's foggy glass.

I roll my window down, lean across my sister
to roll my brother's down.
He slaps my hand, punches my arm.
My sister yelps.

Father tightens his grip on the wheel,
speeds downhill.

We pass through a small country town,
the stores shuttered, sidewalks empty.

I count the cows in pastures—
the cows standing, the ones laying down.

Who are the women who live behind the farmhouse doors?
Who do they talk to?

Skating With My Older Brother in March

There you are in the center
of the pond calling to me.
There's soup cooking at home.
No one knows we're here.

I bend to tie my skates,
pick up mittens wet with slush,
skate the edge, my nylon snowpants
swishing as I try to balance.

Dry grass spikes through
half-frozen ice around me.
I watch small cracks grow,
you skate away.

The Sleeping Porch
for my sister

I

I pull open the sofa—
its creaky springs too tight—
tuck in the muslin sheet,
add a thin blanket while you line up
your stuffed animals.

II

Your bright blonde hair spills across the pillow next to me.
I sleep on the outside so you won't roll off.
The June air's cool, still,
the scattered stars visible through screened windows.

III

Voices down the hallway— secrets—until
I'm asleep too.

IV

We wake to find ourselves on this side
of a long passage, listening to each other.

1963, Fourteen Years Old

The mystery of this flat pattern
creating something curved,
taking the shape of my body.

I watch my mother run seams
through the Singer machine.
Me, ready to catch it
as it comes through.

The Fitting

I'm in stocking feet,
turning slowly clockwise as my mother
pulls straight pins from between her teeth
to adjust the hem on the dress
she's making me.

More pins.
For perfection.

I watch myself in her bedroom mirror—
behind me, her dressmaker dummy, bare, in the corner of the room.

The wool fabric scratches my skin.

I won't tell her I don't like it.

III

The Visit

I walk around to open my mother's door.

We know she won't return.
Two of us alone here,

the tinfoil-wrapped pot
of yellow chrysanthemums in my hands.

The dead don't care about flowers.

I pull my coat against the cold,
watch the slate sky for rain.

Stark quiet,
only the crunch of gravel underfoot.

My mother's jaw tightens.
Can I carry her grief?

We pass a granite cherub,
wings chipped long ago.

At our stone, two small oval pictures
partly hidden by weeds:

grandmother in her flowered headscarf,
grandfather in a shirt and tie.

Mother kneels, pulls at grass,
works to dig the bright flowers

into the cold soil with bare hands.

Leaving My Mother

I kiss her forehead—
too cheerful—
make sure the water pitcher
is within reach, avoid her eyes.

Goodbye happens inch by inch.
Like when you get up in the middle of the night
in a strange house. Small steps.

Oxygen tanks hum through open doors.
Framed anniversary photos on dressers.
Fabric flowers on televisions turned up too high.

I hear my useless words. Little boomerangs
that come back to me in the elevator,
the parking lot as I drive away.

On the highway heading west, I see
a young woman bend to fix my pillow.
She calls me dear, tucks me into bed.
Shuts off the light.

Father Tucked Away

Your clothes are packed.

In the drawer of your nightstand,
a cardbox of pictures.

I study our faces and wonder what part
of my memories I'm dreaming.

Your strong arms are open
as I run towards you.

Both of us are laughing.
There's the smell of newly mown grass.

You toss me in the air,
each of us raising up the other.

Pantoum For My Grandmother

Memory is a garden I enter
to find you digging.
On bended knees and in silence,
the sounds of your trowel, your other language.

I find you digging
as I call to you from behind tall corn.
The sounds of your trowel, your other language.
Won't you dig up words as you work?

As I call to you from behind tall corn,
I wait for you to answer.
Won't you dig up words as you work?
The garden, your meditation,

I wait for you to answer
when, long dead, you come back to me,
the garden your meditation.
I see in your eyes what you cannot say.

When, long dead, you come back to me,
memory is a garden I enter.
I see in your eyes what you cannot say,
on bended knees and in silence.

Friday Morning, Ratíškovice

My four aunties gather in Milka's kitchen.
I sit in my kitchen four thousand miles away.

Stories tumble out as they drink coffee,
shuffle crumbs around the metal table.
Spoons clink chipped mugs. More cream,
sugar. Clear plastic covers the linen cloth
laid for Sunday. Fabric flowers sent twenty years ago
from *Ameriky* sit on the corner of the window sill.

Auntie Ruzena stands, loud, stout, shakes her fist out the window
at the boy on the street below fighting with his friend.
It's a small village. She'll tell his mother.
Jesismaria! She will.

They're all stout. Bakers. Makers of noodles, dumplings, roasts.
I feel their soft arms as I take another sip.

The small mutt groans in the corner, rolls over,
goes back to sleep curled up under the silver radiator
on thin, yellow and black-flecked linoleum.

Marka—the one who tells me I don't visit enough, the one
who says, *this is your home too*—slaps the table.
Another story. Laughter.

I pour one more coffee. Cream and sugar.
Wait.

Old Town Square, Prague

I want to fly up, touch the frescos on my favorite building.
Did I paint them centuries before

when I lived here? Which lifetime am I in
now? These cobblestones, hard to walk on then

as today. I am a child, gawking at the stalls,
my mother's distant voice drifts in and out

from the songs the band plays. These words, these songs
familiar to me.

I pick out three intricately painted eggs
from hundreds in the old woman's stand.

I can't speak fluently to her,
so we use hand gestures, her wrinkled skin

dark from hot fields. Her red flowery babushka
slipping down her long grey hair.

Kathleen Goldblatt (1949-) is a writer and Jungian analyst. She is a training analyst with the CG Jung Institute of New England and the Inter-Regional Society of Jungian Analysts and has been an advocate for social reform, most notably for the mentally ill. She grew up in western New York State, has lived in Boston Massachusetts and resides in Newport, Rhode Island.

www.ingramcontent.com/pod-product-compliance
Lightning Source LLC
Chambersburg PA
CBHW022124090426
42743CB00008B/1000